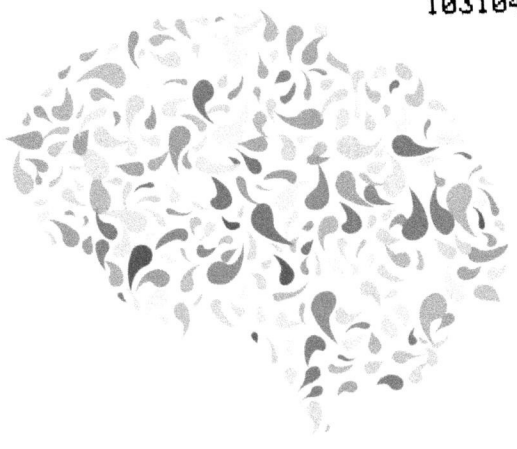

what's in your

THE JOURNEY OF
RESTORING THE
CHATTER IN
YOUR MIND

Sherol "Shugaloo" Cox, MAHL

WHAT'S IN YOUR CHATTERBOX

Copyright © 2021 by Sheree Cox

ISBN: 9780578953427 (paperback)

Cox Consulting & Coaching, LLC
www.payhip.com/shereecox

Book cover designed by Jasmine R. Cox

Publisher: Joseph's Ministry, LLC
www.josephsministryllc.com

Scripture taken from the King James Version. Copyright © 1982 by Thomas Nelson. Used by permission. All rights reserved.

Scripture quotations marked MSG are taken from THE MESSAGE, copyright © 1993, 2002, 2018 by Eugene H. Peterson. Used by permission of NavPress, represented by Tyndale House Publishers. All rights reserved.

Scripture quotations marked (NIV) are taken from The Holy Bible, New International Version®, NIV® Copyright 1973, 1978, 1984, 2011 by Biblica, Inc.™ Used by Permission. All rights reserved worldwide.

All rights reserved. Printed in the United States of America. No part of this book may be used or reproduced in one's business, organization, or lectures without the written permission, except for quotes or referring and giving credit to the author.

DISCLAIMER AND LIMITED LIABILITY:

Although many may find the tools, tips, strategies and/or techniques in the book helpful for their personal growth and professional development, this book is sold with the understanding that the author Sheree Cox is not giving legal, psychological, emotional, or spiritual advice. Nor is this book intended to prescribe cure or diagnosis of any mental or emotional illnesses. Please seek professional help if this book was purchased for that intent. Every person's journey is different, which includes different outcomes and situations. This book promises no form of outcome for any situation and should only be used for empowerment purposes only. The book does not replace professional help, and although the author is a professional educator, trainer, and coach, she does not write with the intent to cure, diagnose, or prescribe any mental or emotional disease. You may reach out to Coach Sheree Cox for additional assistance in one-on-one coaching.

This book shall not be reproduced and/or copied without the written consent of the author of this book.

This book belongs to

_____

I commit to a transformation and renewing of the mind, that I may be a light and blessing to others as well as myself.

Signed,
Loving myself

DEDICATION

To my family, friends, friend-enemies, and in-season individuals who have entered and exited my life, you have ignited and inspired this book. One important lesson I have learned over the years is to know who is in your circle, who is inspiring and motivating you to be all that you are designed to be.

Thank you for the accountability.

I pray, as you read this book, your heart and soul will be soothed, your thoughts clarified, and your mindset will become a powerful source to reckoned with.

Greatness is yours!

Love,

Sheree

TABLE OF CONTENTS

Forward	*11*
What's in your Chatterbox	*13*
1. *What is a Chatterbox*	*15*
2. *Staying In or Move Out the Box*	*21*
3. *Designed for This Journey*	*31*
4. *What Happened? Why am I Here?*	*43*
5. *Back to The Pavement; At What Speed?*	*49*
6. *Discovering The New You*	*63*
7. *It's Time – The Power of Positivity*	*71*
About the Author	*77*

FORWARD

The author has spoken to you in a heartfelt fashion, as we read the words on the pages of this book. I've known Sheree, the author, for a very long time, and as I read the words on the pages of "What's in Your Chatterbox," it has given me a different respect to listening to the lies we tell ourselves. The life of my beautiful friend gives me a new look of the life that we need to have by creating a new path and listening to our inner self through God (Holy Spirit).

In this book, the author has poured her life, the good, the bad, and the not-so-good. In the eyes of our Heavenly Father, we are always forgiven if we know Him and seek Him. My beloved friend gave us a step-by-step process to renew, restore, and rediscover the best in ourselves. This book is a must-read!

The book is designed to give anyone the time to search for your daily purpose in life, have the heart of God, and watch your soul change. As we read and reflect, we can make better choices for the future…but those who have hope in the Lord will renew their strength. They will soar on wings like eagles; they will run and not grow weary; they will walk and not be faint. Isaiah 40:31 (NIV)

Peace and blessing,

Rochelle Alexander

WHAT'S IN YOUR CHATTERBOX

This book will enlighten you on how individuals may only look at the word "chatterbox" in a negative way, but that is not the case, and this author will show you how to determine what your chatterbox looks like. Through the personal experiences of the author, she shares her authentic stories that will have you laughing, crying, and thinking about how you can change a negative thought into a positive one. There are systematic guided steps and self-reflecting moments throughout the book that will empower you to want to develop your personal growth and transform your mindset to a positive outlook, even in your worse learning situations or challenges.

CHAPTER 1
WHAT IS A CHATTERBOX

Chatterbox is defined by dictionary.com to be an excessively talkative person. Now that is to be true in the content of a noun. However, I want you to expand just a little and see a chatterbox of your own voices that enter your mind and thought process, excessively inputting words into your head.

Chatterbox can also be other individuals that you allow to keep you company; that is, in your inner circle. Usually, those are the same voices that are sometimes positive and other times negative. These individuals project the different voices, sometimes heard, however, some are from your own subconscious mind. If you are not careful, you will be weighed down by the negativity filling your box with distraction, despair, and emptiness. BE CAREFUL not to be caught up.

Have you ever had that one friend in your inner circle that had something bad to say about everything and everybody, to the point that no one wants to invite him/her to go anywhere? Be honest, we all have at least one. Well, this is what happens when you stay around in the negative chatter.

I remember a time that my chatterbox was full of gossip and hater-aide. Now you may ask, "What is hater-aide?" Hater-aide is people that talk of the success of others in negative and malicious intentions. (Oxford Dictionary) Just know that you are a part of the hater-aide and gossip even if you do not have an input in the conversation. If you stick around, listen, and engage, you are then guilty as charged. This is called the "negative Nancies" in your circle that are allowed to stay, wherefore we entertain what I like to call "Foolery." (Yourdictionary.com)

If one is not careful and aware, it is easy to become absorbed and drowned by the chatter. Have you ever noticed that as long as you are on a lower platform, your life is full of all the supportive words that they think you want to hear? Well, maybe I am the only one, but I doubt it. The funny thing about that question is that normally, you do not figure that out until you start to rise up the platform of your own success. The expectations for yourself grow larger, therefore, your millions of friends become fewer, and your chatterbox of negative Nancies disappear. The good thing is that you learn how important the positive panties come to fill your chatterbox to a state of overflow with inspiration, motivation, accountability, gratitude, and abundant blessings.

Now, as we continue to press forward on this journey, let's look deep into our chatterbox to identify what is staring back at you and what changes will happen in order to grow in your life.

Isaiah 43:18-19 (NIV)

Forget the former things; do not dwell on the past. See, I am doing a new thing. Now it springs up; do you not perceive it? I am making a way in the wilderness and streams in the wasteland.

*Reflection:*_____

CHAPTER 2
STAYING IN OR MOVING OUT OF THE BOX

Wisdom will tell us that we should know better. Careful, yet rebellious, I am one to admit that I do not always listen. I grew up in a Baptist Church with Christian values, which dictated and formed the life I live today. The thought of having the so-called "bad friends" during my childhood had a negative influence on the decisions that were made, and it was frowned upon by my mother and grandparents. Just think, these were the same type of friends that I was drawing close to, which was the opposite of everything that was poured into me as the foundation of right and wrong. Is it because opposites attract that we battle positive energy versus negative energy?

Good versus bad. Angelic versus demonic. There is something intriguing about doing the very thing that you are told not to do. Why is this? Well, let us move into your Chatterbox, or better yet, let us move into mine.

I was around twelve years old, almost thirteen. There is not much of a difference, you know, especially when you are in the teenage years. I had my first boyfriend, who was four years older than me, so of course, he was filling my head, saying the opposite of what I was taught. This type of communication went on in the relationship off and on through middle school and high school.

Do you remember the time having a best friend that would always co-sign on everything you did even when they were not supposed to? A Bonnie and Clyde friend. YES, it's okay to laugh…we all have them. The question comes, what do you do when every time you turn around, you have this best friend in your ear, co-signing on things that you know aren't best for you? Peer pressure is what it is called. The crazy thing about peer pressure is that it continues to repeat itself as long as you allow it to repeat itself.

Although certain behaviors may have started at twelve years of age for me, one thing is for sure; if I did not stop allowing the pressure to influence me, it would have continued well into my adult life. Thankfully, I learned this one thing early on. So let us not get it twisted. I have always been a leader, but just because you are a leader does not mean you do not experience peer pressure. Ask yourself these questions:

1. Did you think no one would ever know?
2. Did you think it would just go away?
3. Are you happy with your decision?
4. Would you do it all over again?

5. Would you do it all over again, even if you were being watched?

At some point in our lives, we all come to the realization that all of the questions above must be answered and reflected upon. The situations that we put ourselves in and the decisions that we make, directly reflect some of the places we may find ourselves at right now in our lives.

So let us dig a little deeper into my chatterbox, so you will know what not to do. I am now nineteen years of age and married to the same man that I was in a relationship with since I was twelve years old. Crazy in love, and I clearly remember my grandma saying to me, "Baby, you're too young, and that is not the man that God has called you to be with." Of course, my granny's words were null and voided to my ear gate.

It was due to this choice, listening to outsiders who had no great interest for my life, that I moved forward yet backward for two and a half years. In my head, at first, I thought I was doing the right thing, but then I realized that my decisions were based upon negative Nancies in my circle. I had married a drug dealer with no future. Clearly, my decision was not a great one, but it was one out of love. The kind where you think you are bigger than God to change a person and make them better. Yeah, I know, go ahead and laugh; I still do. We have all been there. The time when we did what we wanted to do anyway and then looked back and said, "Why am I here? What was I thinking?" The answer is, sometimes we find ourselves willfully *deceived*.

Deceived defined in Webster dictionary as:

(of a person) cause (someone) to believe something that is not true, typically in order to gain some personal advantage.

- (of a thing) give a mistaken impression. "the area may seem to offer nothing of interest, but don't be deceived."
- fail to admit to oneself that something is true. "enabling the rulers to deceive themselves about the nature of their own rule."

Synonyms:
swindle, defraud, cheat, trick, hoodwink, hoax, dupe, takein, mislead, delude, fool, outwit, misguide, leadon, inveigle, seduce, ensnare, entrap, beguile, double-cross, gull.

Through all of these times of making my own decisions, it was time to deal with what was important, and that was and still is my Heart.

Restore and repair the HEART.

I learned that when God is not in the decision-making process, things will crumble, as it did for my marriage. Let us not be the same anymore, for we hold the power. II Timothy 1:6-7 NIV says, "God gave us not the spirit of fear but gave us love, power, and self-discipline." Now let us move out of a chatterbox and into our destiny.

Now it is time to reflect and revitalize.

Isaiah 40:31 NIV

But those who hope in the LORD will renew their strength. They will soar on wings like eagles; they will run and not grow weary, they will walk and not be faint.

Reflection:

CHAPTER 3
DESIGNED FOR THIS JOURNEY

Have you ever heard the phrase, "You can do it!" or "You got this" or "Girl, you were designed for this"? Well, I want you to take that phrase literally. You are designed to meet any destiny or journey God has set forth for you. The biggest question is, "Are you willing to put in the hard work"?

Have you ever been in the boxing ring with yourself? I have! I want you to know again that you are designed for this journey, so let us get ready to run the race together. Thank God for each day that He has given you air to breathe. Just to run the race to your destiny.

For every individual that is reading this book right now, I pray you will open up your ear gate and hear what the word of God is telling you. I pray every heart, mind, and soul rest on the breastplate of the Lord. In order to get to your destiny, you must first rest with the assurance that God is Almighty, marvelous, and is a loving God to all of His children.

There are times one may ask for patience, not really understanding the depth of the request. When we ask for patience, be prepared for the obstacles, situations, challenges, and things that are beyond your control to come before us to develop our patience. Do not forget that is the TEST! We must confess that we all do right and wrong things from time to time; however, we are given grace and mercy in our lives today, tomorrow, and forevermore.

I do not know about you, but I often wonder if God thinks that these are my children that I uniquely designed for a purpose. Will they run the race to their destiny? The answer He wants is yes, so I say to you, meet me on the field and let us run. We have work to do.

Walk or Talk

There is a saying, "Walk the walk," that some people use all day long, while others just talk the talk. When will you run the race? Often times, it has been one, two, five, or even ten years have passed. So, now are you ready to run?

When we are born into the world, we squirmed and scooted around, and learned to rock back and forward. Before long, we began crawling around, and after a while, we were balancing and standing. Before you knew it, we were taking our first steps. As our physical parents were patient, excited, and proud of our learning, so is God.

Do you remember parents saying, "that is my big girl or my big boy?" How much enthusiasm was in their voice? Continuously working on us in our "Walk of Life," He expects us to intelligently grow just as our physical parents do. You can choose to walk with God; it's fine if you want to stay in the same place in your current life. God is on the move, and if you want to keep up, you must run the race.

Psalms 4-7 NIV teaches our children about the praises unto the Lord and about His power. They will know, trust, and obey God for themselves. Have you ever been in a situation that you know God's patience is running thin with you? Well, I am going to be honest. I have been in that situation where there is a feeling that time is about to run out and you must do what you have been called to do no matter how hard it seems. The reality is, you are designed for the journey, whatever it may be. Just take the Nike slogan, "Just do it." God is always there to guide you if you fall, and His hand is there to pick you up.

I want you in this chapter to stop and go look in the mirror and tell yourself you are running this race and you will finish. I am laughing because I had to ask myself the same question when writing this book. The funny thing is, if you go out on faith and have God in your life, then running the race is fun. I can tell there is nothing more enlightening than running the race and seeing your destiny fulfilled.

Experiences take too long to get to your destiny, walking will get you there eventually, and some of you may think it is not my time. My sister, my brother, I say to you, then take a brisk walk and elevate your steps to running. I looked up the word brisk on freedictionary.com, and it said, "marked by speed, liveliness, and vigor; energetic." This is a time our Father is not standing still, waiting on us to catch up. Those days are gone. You are prepared and trained for the battlefield; no need for fear of what possibilities will occur. Finishing the race will elevate you in a way that no man can tear you down.

One day, I remember asking myself what this journey will look like. Why can't I have self-accountability? The fact of the matter is, we can look for other people to help us to be accountable for the things related to our life, but remember, this is your journey. The journey that God has designed for you. Do you think that God would have designed a unique journey for you and not equip you with the proper tools? In Matthew 17:20 NIV it says, "if you have faith as small as a mustard seed, you can move a mountain", therefore a little faith is enough to hold on to for your own accountability. When accountability kicks in, your mindset changes permanently as you move on the road of righteousness; as it pertains to fulling the goals you had sitting on the shelf and goals for the future. Just remember you are equipped with enough.

The word of God tells us, no weapon that is formed against us shall prosper. (Isaiah 54:17 KJV) Let us dive into that for a moment carefully. He did not say that the weapons would not be formed; it is just that they will not prosper against us. The feelings of anxiety, fear and/or hesitation may form as a negative feeling; however, there's no need to allow these feelings to consume you into believing you cannot fulfill your journey.

Manifest your vision or your journey. One may ask, how do I fulfill my journey? How do I get started? Here we go: First, believe in yourself and stop waiting on others to believe in you. What I mean by this is, there are individuals in your face putting hatea-raid all around your vision. Second, you have to make a plan on how you will fulfill the vision. The word of God says in Habakkuk 2: 2 KJV, "Write the vision and make it plain on tablets that he may run when reading it." Therefore, you will need to write down the step-by-step process of how you will fulfill each vision, each goal, and each journey. Third, take your time and organize. You do not have the ability to tackle everything at one time unless you are looking for chaos or failure. Remember, we are a spirit that dwells within a human body. Fourth, apply yourself and be diligent and faithful to the things that you say you are going to do. If it does not work the first, second, third, fourth, or even fifth time, do not give up. Keep pressing forward, even when you do not want to because there will be those days. Real talk!

Now, let us meditate on this scripture as you reflect on the journey for your life.

James 3:17 (NIV)

But the wisdom from above is first of all pure. It is also peace loving, gentle at all times, and willing to yield to others. It is full of mercy and the fruit of good deeds. It shows no favoritism and is always sincere.

Reflection:

CHAPTER 4
WHAT HAPPENED? WHY AM I HERE?

Welcome back! You thought that you had it all together and doing your thing. Right? Well, join me in helping you to understand why you are here again. Sometimes, we lose focus on our vision, wherefore you get entangled with the dreams and perspectives of what others think you should do. These situations happen more often than we would like to admit to ourselves. Fear seems to be the number one factor in going backwards; however, God has not given us the Spirit of Fear.

Repeat after me:

For the weapon of war is the Word of God. I shall not let the enemy's distractions woo me into being outside of my character in who I am. For I know that no matter what, this battle of war is already won, for the Holy Spirit dwells within me.

I would like to share this short story with you because there is wisdom and knowledge that is bestowed in you, wherefore now is the time to retract to get on track.

I had a situation where money was stolen by a family member, and in a split second, I almost went backward into my old self. For me, to be able to mirror what my old self, out of character, would have done was absolutely crazy. Instead, I felt heartbroken, disturbed, in unbelief, disappointed, but I did not react. I did not allow my emotions to take over. I had to decide at that very moment to let no man or women stand in my way of what needed to get done. I literally had to speak life into myself and say, "I am what God says I am." What does God say you are? What do you think or say you are? Are you standing on what God says you are? Or are you standing on your own words? You are back here because of your mindset. Procrastinating or stalling on parts of your vision put you back here again. Today, I want you to declare and decree that you will be all that God has called you to be and will stay on purpose.

Start your day with I am <u>Uniquely Awesome.</u>

More examples may be:

·I am a _____

·I am a _____

·I am a _____

Be still and allow the word of God to meditate into your heart that you may grow like a flower, wherefore your roots are embedded into the Word of

God. Now, I want you to imagine an oak tree full grown with roots growing under the foundation of a house. Sometimes, what happens is the roots break up the foundation of a house and cause damage, which brings destruction and discord. This is what happens in our lives when we decide to go in our own direction, down our own path. Understand that God gives us choice, and when altered what He has designed for us, then you can only be upset with yourself when things do not turn out as you thought they were to.

Reflect on what choices you made out of hast. Write down what you could have done differently.

_____

_____

_____

_____

_____

CHAPTER 5

BACK TO THE PAVEMENT... AT WHAT SPEED?

In this chapter, we talked about how you went backwards to where you were before. However, that is a lesson for you to move forward. I did not want to spend much time talking about the old or the past. It is time to move forward. The question is, at what speed are you moving forward...slow with procrastination, mid-speed walking, or taking off running? I would hope that you are fired up to start running the race at full speed. Are you wondering what that looks like? Well, let me show you how to pick up the pace.

First, understand that the road you take that is with God will take you on a journey that you would never imagine. That is a good thing. As you start to transition into a more active role in your destiny, you will begin to own your truth; dig deep within yourself to win at a record speed.

Ask yourself these four questions and be very honest.

1. What is holding you back? Answer: _____

Example: fear, anxiety, depression, unorganized, forgiveness, procrastination, worry

Read and reflect before you move on:

Proverbs 12:24-25 (NIV)

Anxiety weighs down the heart, but a kind word cheers it up. The righteous choose their friends carefully, but the way of the wicked leads them astray.

***Reflection*:**

2. When should I start my new journey? Answer: <u>NOW!</u>

Read and reflect before you move on:

Philippians 4:6-7 (MSG)

Do not fret or worry. Instead of worrying, pray. Let petitions and praises shape your worries into prayers, letting God know your concerns. Before you know it, a sense of God's wholeness, everything coming together for good, will come and settle you down. It is wonderful what happens when Christ displaces worry at the center of your life.

Reflection:

3. How will you move into your new journey?

_____

Determine the root causes that make you feel out of control or have unwired emotions. Whatever it is, FACE IT head-on. For this example, I will use fear because that was my truth. Fear of succeeding, therefore, I had to call out my fears, deal and conquer it first. This is how you change your mindset, by taking action in declaring and decreeing the word of God over your life. Repeat after me.

a. I declare and decree that I am choosing to be free from all the negative afflictions in my life holding me down.

b. I declare and decree that I who God says I am. Speak what that is for you…

c. I declare and decree that I am whole and shackle free.

Read and reflect before you move on:

Psalms 51:10 (KJV)

Create in me a clean heart, O God; and renew a right spirit within me.

Reflection:

4. How will I hold myself accountable?

_____

First, understand that you must need and want to change; therefore, you will look to hold yourself accountable. All others are just the extra support you need when feeling a little weak. Pray and ask God for guidance and strength. You are never alone on your journey.

Matthew 6:33 (NIV)

But seek first his kingdom and his righteousness, and all these things will be given to you as well.

Reflection:

CHAPTER 6
DISCOVERING THE NEW YOU

The most important and greatest adventure is discovering who you really are. Discovering or finding yourself may sound like an inherently self-centered goal, but in actuality, it is an unselfish process to get to the root of everything you do in life.

1. Make sense of your past because the attitudes and atmosphere that you grew up in have a heavy hand on how you act as adults. The painful early life experiences often determine how you define and defend yourselves. They bend you out of shape, influencing behaviors in ways in which you are hardly aware.

2. Differentiate is simplified by Dr. Firestone that wrote, "To lead a free life, a person must separate him/herself from negative imprinting and remain open and vulnerable."
3. Seek Meaning is understanding you must seek out your own personal sense of purpose. This means separating your own point of view from other people's expectations of you. In addition, it means asking yourselves what your values are, what truly matters, then following the principles you believe in.
4. Think about what you want; it may sound simple but knowing what you want is fundamental to finding yourselves. Being able to recognize your wants and desires helps you to realize who you are and what is important to you.
5. Recognize that your personal power means that you challenge taking power over your life.

No longer are you engaging in a spiral of negative thoughts or thinking that tells you all the things that are wrong with the world around or all the reasons you cannot have what you want. Instead, accept yourself as a powerful player in your own destiny. Harnessing your personal power is essential to both finding and becoming yourselves. Personal power is based on your strength, confidence, and competency as you develop a positive mindset.

6. Silence your inner critic with the judgmental attitude that tells you that you are not good enough to succeed or you don't deserve what you want. The negative process is destructive, and by recognizing and standing up to this internal enemy, you can disarm negative thoughts.

7. Practice compassion and generosity. They are mental health principles that one should practice no matter what. Enough said.

8. Know the value of friendship. They are those who support that light that dwells inside of you; the light that shines and inspires you to feel passionate about life. Being able to have a support system that believes in you, helps you to realize your goals and develop your potentials. Remember, you do not need many people in your corner; one will suffice. Do not overthink the process of friends in your corner; it is not worth the time.

Stepping out into the positive Chatterbox means changing your circle, changing your thought process, changing your mindset, and changing your habits. One must be able to have the ability and the willingness to be uncomfortable, willing to stretch forth and press forward.

Sometimes, we mistakenly think of self-understanding as self-indulgence, and we carry on without asking the most important question one will ever ask: Who am I *really*? Now, look in the mirror. What does that look like for you? All of the great affirmations and positive quotes sound well, but what I can tell you is, it is a challenge. The challenge lies in restoring and transforming your mindset. So here we go:

1. Create a list of your friends and family. Then, by their names, write P for positive or N for negative.
2. Look at that same list and identify your haters and put them out.
3. Put a checkmark by your motivators, your supporters, those that inspire you.
4. Locate four scriptures and or quotes for each week of the month that will help you to move permanently out of your negative chatterbox.

Here are some examples:

- Romans 8:6 KJV, "For to be carnally minded is death, but to be spiritually minded is life and peace."
- Luke 11: 36 KJV, "If thy whole body therefore be full of light, having no part dark, the whole shall be full of light, as when the bright shining of a candle doth give thee light."
- Galatians 6:9 NIV, "Let us not grow weary while doing good, for in due season we shall reap if we do not lose heart."
- My own quote, "Enjoy walking in the valley; you will appreciate the destination more."

Take your list with your checkmark and build you an inner circle on the mountaintop while nesting your egg, whatever that may be. Your new inner circle will help to nurture and protect your egg until it is ready to be born. Finally, soar like an eagle. Greatness is yours, so go take it.

CHAPTER 7
IT'S TIME...
THE POWER OF POSITIVITY

Remember, chatter is negative and positive, and it is up to you to determine whether yours is positive or negative. Transformation does not just happen. It is all about the journey one decides to take, which takes work and consistency. That is why a step-by-step process is needed to move into a positive mindset, which is designed especially for you.

This is now the time in your life that you will begin to outline the new you and press forward with what you want for yourself. This is your time to be intentional with your transformation into the positive pansy I know you are.

Who am I?

_____
_____
_____
_____
_____
_____
_____

Who do people think I am and why? (Is that a good or bad thing?)

_____
_____
_____
_____
_____
_____

What do I want to change about myself and/or challenge myself?

When will I start?

___

How will I hold myself accountable?

_____

_____

_____

_____

_____

_____

_____

_____

_____

_____

_____

At the end of each day, compliment yourself, for you are designed to be great.

    Love,

    Minister Sheree Cox

ABOUT THE AUTHOR

Sheree Cox is a wife, mother, ordained minister, educator, transformational coach, and holds a graduate degree from Liberty University in Management & Leadership. She has co-authored three Amazon best-seller books: The Purposed Women 365 Day Devotional, Powerful Principles of the Beauty CEO, and Daily Dose of Declarations: 365 Positive Affirmations.

Sheree is the CEO/Founder of Grassroot Connections, a non-profit organization that focuses on building a foundation of family success through learning self-sufficiency, women empowerment, and outreach ministries (including the homeless population of Charlotte and Concord, North Carolina).

Mrs. Cox is also the CEO of two other companies, ReeSunshine Nail and Beauty Spa, which provides an experience for individuals to be relaxed, restored, and renewed in their minds while being pampered. Secondly, The Cox Consulting & Coaching Company, which consults and coaches individuals in their personal life and business venues from vision to victories.

Her expertise in Human and Social services allowed active engagement for more than 18 years of assisting families and children. Since 2010, Sheree has mentored at-risk mothers, youth entrepreneurship and facilitated women's empowerment workshops and seminars throughout Charlotte, NC, and Miami, FL. Her non-profit organization has continuously provided outreach services to more than 200 homeless individuals annually.

Grassroot Connections is currently partnered with Institutions Mixte Petits Poussins de Beauge

School in Port-a- Prince, Haiti, building a school library named "The Build- to- Read Library," which cultivates and nurtures the young children of Haiti the opportunity to fluently speak English as a second language.

www.ingramcontent.com/pod-product-compliance
Lightning Source LLC
Chambersburg PA
CBHW071839290426
44109CB00017B/1871